REEL COWBOYS

Western movie stars who thrilled young fans and helped them grow up decent and strong

By

Bill O'Neal

EAKIN PRESS Austin, Texas

FIRST EDITION

Published in the United States of America
By Eakin Press
A Division of Sunbelt Media, Inc.
P.O. Drawer 90159 ✉ Austin, Texas 78709-0159
email: eakinpub@sig.net
website: www.eakinpress.com

2 3 4 5 6 7 8 9

1-57168-330-0

Library of Congress Cataloging-in-Publication Data

O'Neal, Bill.
Reel Cowboys: western movie stars who thrilled young fans and helped them grow up decent and strong/ by Bill O'Neal.
p. cm.
Includes bibliographical references and index.
ISBN 1-57168-330-0
1. Western Films--History and criticism. 2. Motion picture actors and actresses--United States Biography. 3. Television actors and actresses--United States Biography. I. Title
PN1995.9.W4054 2000
791.43'028'092273--dc21 99-15816
[B] CIP

For my littlest cowgirl,
Chloe Celeste Martinez.

Monte Hale and Partner

Contents

Roy Rogers and Trigger

Cowboy Heroes

They Fought for What Was Right

When I was a boy I saw Western movies every week. There were five theaters in my hometown of Corsicana, Texas. Each theater changed movies three times a week, and many of those movies were Westerns.

I would go to the movies on Saturdays and sometimes after school. On Saturdays I would see a double feature—two movies for the price of one. Children's admission was only nine cents.

In those days, children all over America watched Western heroes battle outlaws every week. There were fistfights and shootouts and galloping horseback chases. The cowboy heroes protected pretty women and children and elderly people. Cowboy heroes were brave and strong and always did the right thing. Cowboy heroes were handsome, too. They could ride and shoot and fight. Some of them—the "Singing Cowboys"—could also sing and play a guitar.

My favorite cowboy heroes were John Wayne, Roy Rogers, Gene Autry, Randolph Scott, and Gary Cooper. In earlier years, boys and girls had their own screen idols: Tom Mix, Hoot Gibson, Ken Maynard, Buck Jones, and other hard-riding stars.

Many of these great movie heroes were also heroic in real life. Tom Mix joined the army during the Spanish-American War. Hoot Gibson and Fred Thomson volunteered for military service in World War I. Col. Tim McCoy served in both World War I and World War II. Buck Jones died trying to rescue friends from a fire. Gene Autry and James Stewart were pilots during World War II. Stewart later was promoted to general in the U.S. Air Force. Audie Murphy won the Medal of Honor and was the most decorated soldier in World War II.

On the movie screen, these cowboy heroes fought the forces of evil. They told stories of brave pioneers in the Wild West. Their movies were exciting and fun to watch. And through watching their movies, children learned right from wrong. Cowboy heroes helped boys and girls grow up with a strong sense of values. Kids grew up wanting to be like their heroes.

I hope you enjoy reading about the Western stars who meant so much to so many boys and girls, and helped us all grow up to be decent and strong.

Silent Film Stars

The Great Train Robbery caused a sensation in 1903. It was a one-reel film, about ten minutes long. *The Great Train Robbery* told the story of a Western outlaw gang that robbed a train. The gang celebrated in a saloon, but a posse chased down the train robbers and killed them. Audiences were thrilled over this exciting little movie, even if there was no sound.

Outlaw gangs were still robbing trains in the West in 1903. Audiences loved *The Great Train Robbery* and wanted more.

Broncho Billy Anderson, who acted in *The Great Train Robbery*, began to film one-reelers. These short movies could be filmed in a few days. There was a new Broncho Billy Anderson movie every week for years. Broncho Billy became the first movie star.

The next great Western star was William S. Hart. Hart had lived in the West. His movies brought the look of the real West to the screen.

Audiences like movies with action, and Westerns filled the screen with galloping horses and magnificent scenery. Other Western stars of silent films were fine athletes who could ride and fight. Talented rodeo performers such as Tom Mix and Hoot Gibson became the greatest silent Western stars.

Broncho Billy Anderson

Broncho Billy Anderson
The First Movie Star

One of the actors in *The Great Train Robbery* was twenty-one-year-old G. M. Anderson. Because of the sensational success of *The Great Train Robbery*, Anderson wanted to make more Western movies. Within a few years Anderson and George Spoor formed a company to make films. They named their company Essanay. Essanay was one of the first companies to film in California.

In 1908 Anderson began to direct Western movies. Since he could not find a good cowboy actor, Anderson himself played the hero in his Westerns. He had learned to ride horses on a Texas ranch. Because he was husky and strong, he was believable in the fight scenes.

Anderson's first Westerns, like *The Great Train Robbery*, were one-reelers lasting about ten minutes. Soon he expanded to two-reelers, about twenty minutes long.

Anderson began to call his hero "Broncho Billy." Then the name was added to the movie titles: *Broncho Billy's Narrow Escape*, *Broncho Billy's Brother*, *Why Broncho Billy Left Bear Country*, *Broncho Billy's Bible*, and many others.

A new Broncho Billy movie was filmed every week. Some theaters ran only Broncho Billy movies. Fans could hardly wait from week to week for the next exciting Broncho Billy adventure.

From 1908 to 1915 Anderson starred in 375 Westerns. Then he broke off his partnership with Spoor, which stopped him from acting in films for two years.

The public soon forgot Broncho Billy. William S. Hart and Tom Mix had become the most popular Western stars. But the first movie star had been Broncho Billy Anderson.

William S. Hart

William S. Hart
And Fritz

William S. Hart was raised in the Old West. He grew up in Dakota Territory during the 1860s and 1870s. Bill saw cowboys and Native American Sioux. He saw gunfights and cattle drives. Later he would remember the towns and clothing and equipment of the real West. And when Bill became a great movie star, he brought the Old West back to life in his films.

When Bill was fifteen the family moved east to New York City. He was a fine athlete in school, but after leaving school he became a stage actor. He acted in many plays by William Shakespeare. His favorite roles, though, were in Western plays, such as *The Virginian*, *The Squaw Man*, and *Trail of the Lonesome Pine*.

While touring with a play in Cleveland, Ohio, Bill saw his first Western movie. Although he had acted onstage for more than twenty years, he now decided to make Western films.

Bill went to Hollywood, where he found work in films. In 1914 he made his first Western film, *On the Night Stage*. Movie fans loved the Westerns of William S. Hart. His films began as short one- and two-reelers, but soon expanded to hour-long features. Hart directed many of his Westerns.

The first Western movies had been filmed by men from the East. William S. Hart was the first Westerner to make Western films. The dusty towns in his films looked like towns from the Old West. The costumes of the actors in his films looked like Western clothing. The characters in his films acted and reacted like real Westerners.

Hart loved horses. He understood the close comradeship between cowboys and their horses. In 1914 he began using a beautiful pinto named Fritz in his movies. Fritz was intelligent and performed many tricks. Fritz was the first horse to become a movie star.

Hart often played a bad man who was reformed by God or by a pretty woman. He was an honest and religious man, and his movie characters were brave and tough. From 1914 to 1925 Hart filmed more than sixty Westerns.

But in the 1920s the taste of moviegoers changed. Audiences liked the flashy, fast-paced Westerns of Tom Mix. Hart did not want to change the simple, sentimental plots of his films. Now in his fifties, William S. Hart retired from movies.

Hart lived on Horseshoe Ranch, where he wrote Western novels. He brought his beloved horse, Fritz, to his California ranch. When Fritz died, Hart buried him beneath a stone marker on Horseshoe Ranch.

In 1939 his last film, *Tumbleweeds*, was re-released. At Horseshoe Ranch, Hart filmed an eight-minute introduction to *Tumbleweeds*. He talked fondly about the excitement and the hardships of making early Westerns. Then the old star exclaimed, "Oh, the thrill of it all!"

William S. Hart comforts a young actress.

Hoot Gibson
The Hooter

Hoot Gibson was a real cowboy.

He was born Edmund Richard Gibson in Nebraska in 1892. As a boy he began working on ranches. He became an excellent horseman and an expert with a rope.

When he was a teenager his mother moved to California. While visiting his mother, he worked for the Owl Drug Company. His friends began to call him "hoot owl," and his famous nickname soon was shortened to "Hoot."

Hoot Gibson traveled as a performer in Wild West shows. As early as 1910 he worked as a stuntman in Western movies. In 1912 Hoot entered a rodeo in Pendleton, Oregon. He won a silver-plated saddle and a trophy naming him All-Around Champion Cowboy.

In Hollywood Hoot continued to work in movies as a stuntman and trick roper. Hoot was a spectacular rider, and his movie roles became larger.

But just as he was becoming a popular movie star, the United States entered World War I. Hoot abandoned his movie career to volunteer for military service. He was stationed in France with the U.S. Tank Corps.

When Hoot returned to Hollywood after the war, he became a Western superstar. He starred in forty silent films in 1920.

Hoot Gibson movies featured exciting horsemanship and a lot of humor. Hoot tried tricking villains instead of shooting them. Often Hoot did not even wear a gun. If he needed a gun he would borrow one from another character in the movie.

Offscreen Hoot loved to have fun. He enjoyed Hollywood parties.

Hoot Gibson

He rode motorcycles, drove expensive cars, and flew in his own airplane. He became known as the "Hooter."

Hoot's popularity continued when talkies replaced silent films. He made more than 225 movies. At his peak he earned $14,500 per week, and he became a millionaire.

As late as the 1940s, Hoot co-starred in Westerns with Ken Maynard and Bob Steele. Hoot's last appearance in a Western was with his friend John Wayne in the 1959 cavalry film *The Horse Soldiers*.

Hoot Gibson died in 1962 at the age of seventy.

Fred Thomson

Fred Thomson

The Reverend

Fred Thomson was a preacher, a Boy Scout leader, and a champion athlete. In his Western movies he presented wholesome, Christian values, which helped him become one of the greatest stars of silent films.

Fred was born in 1890 at Pasadena, California. His father was a Presbyterian minister. Fred was a gifted athlete who earned college letters in football, basketball, baseball, and track. In 1910 and again in 1911 Fred won first place in the National Track and Field competition. In 1913 Fred shattered track and field records set by the great Jim Thorpe.

Fred earned two college degrees and became a Presbyterian minister in Los Angeles. In 1915 Fred moved to a church in Goldfield, Nevada. He was appointed Nevada's commissioner of Boy Scouts.

But in 1916 Fred's young wife died of a sudden illness. Fred decided to join the U.S. Army as the chaplain of an artillery regiment. When World War I started, Fred and his regiment went to France.

After the war, Fred married again. His new wife was a Hollywood screenwriter. Fred's Hollywood connections, his splendid physique, and his good looks propelled him into the movies.

Fred decided to make Westerns which featured a spectacular horse. He found a wild stallion at a riding school in New York. Fred was able to handle this superb animal. He bought the horse and named him Silver King. Then he took Silver King to California to be trained.

Silver King would be given scenes to show off his intelligence. The big horse performed tricks and sometimes rescued Fred. One movie was titled *Silver King Comes Through*. Young fans loved both Silver King and the handsome Fred Thomson.

Fred and Silver King began starring in Westerns in 1923. The first Fred Thomson Westerns were filmed on Poverty Row. But Fred's films were so popular that he soon was paid $100,000 for each movie.

Fred's last movie, *Kit Carson*, was about a real-life Western hero. Sound was beginning to take over the movie industry, but Fred Thomson would not live to make a talkie.

In December 1928 Fred stepped on a rusty nail. Even though his foot became sore, he did not see a doctor. He became infected with blood poisoning and died on Christmas Day. Fred Thomson was only thirty-eight when he died.

Tom Mix

The Greatest Silent Star

Tom Mix brought the Western to new heights of excitement. Tom had dark good looks and a dazzling smile. He was a flashy dresser with fancy Western costumes. Tom Mix movies were packed with fistfights and hard riding. He became the greatest Western star of the silent screen.

Thomas Edwin Mix was born in 1880 in Mix Run, Pennsylvania. Tom's father drove a carriage and ran the stables for a wealthy man. From his father Tom learned to handle horses and to love animals. "Dad could do anything with a horse," said Tom, "except make him speak."

When Tom was ten he saw a performance of Buffalo Bill Cody's Wild West Show. Tom was so excited that he decided to become a cowboy.

In 1898, when Tom was eighteen, the United States went to war with Spain. Tom enlisted in the U.S. Army. He was assigned to work with horses, but he was never sent overseas to fight.

After Tom left the army, he found work with Wild West shows. At first he handled horses, but he was such a good rider that he began to entertain audiences. While working in Oklahoma with the Miller Brothers 101 Wild West Show, Tom performed with Hoot Gibson. Both Tom and Hoot soon would be Western movie stars.

By 1910 Tom was a deputy sheriff at Dewey, Oklahoma. In that year a movie producer named William Selig was in Oklahoma to film a one-reel documentary about ranching. Tom was hired to help.

Selig was impressed with Tom's riding, roping, and shooting skills. For the next two years Tom made short films for Selig. In 1912 Tom left Selig to work in rodeos. But twice Tom was badly injured in rodeo accidents. He returned to Selig in 1913 to make one- and two-reel Westerns. In 1915 Tom starred in fifty-one films.

Tom Mix and Tony, "The Wonder Horse"

Tom had a magnetic screen presence. He performed all of his own stunts, riding, roping, and fighting at a furious pace. Tom liked to include scenes with speeding trains. He used a lot of comedy.

In 1917 Tom went to work for a larger studio owned by William Fox. The budgets for his films were much bigger. Instead of short one- or two-reel movies, Tom starred in hour-long features.

In his Fox movies, Tom began to wear spectacular costumes—stitched boots, tight pants, fancy shirts, ten-gallon hats. During his career he gave away hundreds of big, white hats. Tom always wore gloves because his hands were soft and he had to handle reins for long hours of filming.

When Tom went to Fox, his horse, Old Blue, was injured and died. Tom already had bought and trained a strong, intelligent chestnut named Tony. He was billed as "Tony, the Wonder Horse." Tom's new horse became so popular that he received fan mail. One letter was addressed, "Just Tony, Somewhere in the U.S.A." Postmen knew Tony, too, and the letter arrived at Tom's ranch.

By 1920 Tom Mix had replaced William S. Hart as the most popular movie cowboy. Tom was paid $17,500 a week. His movies made so much money that Twentieth Century Fox was called "The House That Mix Built."

Tom bought a ranch in Arizona and a mansion in Hollywood. But he also built Mixville, a sixty-acre movie set where many of his Westerns were filmed.

Tom galloped through more than 300 movies filled with daredevil stunts. He regularly exercised to be able to keep up the furious pace of his films. But he had broken many bones, and he was nearly fifty when sound came to movies. In 1928 Tom decided to retire from film work.

Universal Studio, however, was convinced that Tom Mix would continue to be popular in talkies. Tom was persuaded to sign. He made nine movies in 1932, and fans flocked to see Tom Mix.

Exhausted, Tom retired again. He organized his own Wild West show and enjoyed performing in front of live audiences. In 1935 Tom made a final film, a fifteen-part serial called *The Miracle Rider*. During the 1930s a highly popular radio program, *The Tom Mix Show*, used his name but not his voice.

In 1940 Tom was killed in an automobile accident. He was sixty when he died. Tom Mix was the dominant Western star of his lifetime.

The Stars and Their Horses

William S. Hart	Fritz
Fred Thomson	Silver King
Tom Mix	Tony
Ken Maynard	Tarzan
Buck Jones	Silver
Col. Tim McCoy	Pal
Johnny Mack Brown	Rebel
Charles Starrett	Raider
Gene Autry	Champion
Tex Ritter	White Flash
Roy Rogers	Trigger
Dale Evans	Buttermilk
Monte Hale	Partner
Rex Allen	Koko
James Stewart	Pie

Stars of the 1930s and 1940s

Western movies became even better when sound was added. Some of the stars of silent Westerns continued to be popular in the talkies of the 1930s. Tom Mix, Ken Maynard, Buck Jones, and Col. Tim McCoy made the switch from silent to sound Westerns. Their action-packed movies still delighted audiences.

Many new actors became Western stars during the 1930s and 1940s. Bob Steele and his young friend John Wayne began to make B Westerns. Charles Starrett was a new star of B Westerns. Starrett was especially popular as the black-masked "Durango Kid."

Other B Western stars included Wild Bill Elliott, Johnny Mack Brown, Allan "Rocky" Lane, Don "Red" Barry, Monte Hale, and Sunset Carson. William Boyd starred as "Hopalong Cassidy."

These actors filmed hundreds of Westerns a year. Boys and girls learned lessons of right and wrong from the Western stars of the 1930s and 1940s, and generations of young fans would thrill to the adventures of their heroes.

Ken Maynard

Ken Maynard
Co-Starring Tarzan

For twenty years Ken Maynard thrilled Western movie fans. The former rodeo star was an incredible horseman. His movies were filled with exciting riding feats. Ken's horse, Tarzan, was intelligent and well-trained. Tarzan appeared in most of Ken's movies.

Ken was born in 1895 in Indiana. When he was twelve he ran away to join a Wild West show. Ken's father brought him home. But when Ken was sixteen he left home for good. He joined a carnival, then began performing in Wild West shows. Ken learned trick riding and roping.

During World War I, Ken joined the U.S. Army. After the war, Ken returned to Wild West shows. He had become such a skilled cowboy that he entered the rodeo at Pendleton, Oregon. There Ken won $42,000 and a trophy as All-Around Champion Cowboy of the World. The next year he won again.

In 1921 Ken was hired by the Ringling Brothers Barnum and Bailey Circus. He earned $40,000 as the star cowboy of this famous circus. Ken would always love circus life.

But in 1923 Tom Mix gave him a small part in a movie. By 1925 Ken was starring in his own Westerns. Audiences were amazed at his daredevil riding tricks. One of Ken's favorite tricks had been learned when he worked in the circus. He would stand on the backs of two horses and ride them at a gallop. Sometimes he rode four or even six horses that way. Ken was always filmed in closeup, so that fans would know that he performed his own tricks.

When Ken became a movie star, he bought a big palomino. Ken named his new horse "Tarzan" after the popular jungle hero. Tarzan easily learned tricks. Ken put scenes in his movies to show off Tarzan's abilities.

Tarzan would rescue Ken from outlaws, Native American warriors, burning buildings, or quicksand. Tarzan could ring a fire bell, roll over and play dead, nod his head when asked a question, bow down, and dance. One of Ken's movies was titled *Come On, Tarzan*. Tarzan was called "The Wonder Horse" (the same nickname used for Tom Mix's horse, Tony). Tarzan had his own fan club.

In later years the dazzling riding stunts performed by Ken and Tarzan were used in the movies of other stars. Film of these stunts was cut from Ken's old movies and sold to other studios. The stars of these new movies dressed like Ken and rode a horse like Tarzan, so that the stunts would match the other parts of the movie. Even young John Wayne used film clips of Ken and Tarzan in his early movies.

When sound came to movies, Ken became an even bigger star. He worked for a studio that used large budgets for his films. Ken could spend $75,000 to $80,000 on each of his movies. Ken Maynard movies were filmed on location in beautiful areas all over the West.

In his early sound movies Ken began to use cowboy music. Ken sang and played the fiddle. Although he was not a great musician, he was one of the first stars to use music in Western films.

Ken's younger brother, Kermit, appeared in some of his films. Kermit was a good stuntman. Later Kermit starred in his own Westerns.

Tarzan died in 1940, after making the movie *Lightning Strikes West*. Ken made movies for a few years without Tarzan, but it was not the same. After he quit the movie business, Ken worked for years in circuses and rodeos. His fans were always glad to see him.

Ken died in 1973 at the age of seventy-seven.

Buck Jones
A True Hero

Buck Jones was one of the best-liked men in Hollywood. He was admired for his strong sense of right and wrong. Buck played a hero in more than 150 movies. And he proved to be a real hero, dying while trying to rescue friends from a fire.

His real name was Charles Frederick Gebhart. He was born in 1891 in Vincennes, Indiana. While working at a livery stable in Vincennes, the youngster learned to handle horses.

Watching him work with horses, the men around the stable called him "Buckaroo." This nickname was shortened to "Buck." When Buck became a movie actor, he changed his last name to Jones.

Buck wanted adventure. When he was fifteen he joined the United States Cavalry. Buck was too young to enlist, but his mother changed his birthdate so that he could become a soldier.

In the Philippines Buck was badly wounded in the leg. But he re-enlisted in 1910. He wanted to become a pilot in the new Army Air Force, but they would not let Buck fly planes. Buck left the army in 1913 in Texas.

Buck was hired to handle horses by the Miller Brothers 101 Ranch Wild West Show, which was then appearing in Texas. Buck soon became a trick rider in the show.

In 1914 Buck met a young rider named Odille Osborne. She was called Dell, and Buck fell in love with her. In 1915 Buck and Dell were married while mounted on horseback at their show.

Buck and Dell performed for several Wild West shows and circuses. In 1917 they were with the famous Ringling Brothers Circus in California when Dell became pregnant. They decided that they would settle down in California. A baby girl was born and named Maxine.

Buck easily found work as a stuntman in Western films. Then he was given small parts in the films of Tom Mix and other Western stars.

Buck was handsome and rugged. He was a fine rider and looked good on a horse. In 1920 he starred in the first Buck Jones movie, *The Last Straw*.

Buck Jones was an immediate hit. His films were filled with action. Buck read Western novels to find ideas for his movies. During the 1920s, he became as popular as Tom Mix, Hoot Gibson, and Ken Maynard. Boys and girls across the nation joined his fan club, the Buck Jones Rangers.

In 1929 Buck used his life's savings to start the Buck Jones Wild West Show. Everywhere the show played, large crowds gathered. But Buck's business manager was dishonest, and the show went broke.

Buck Jones draws a gun on a "heavy."

In order to pay off his debts, Buck returned to making movies. Although there were no more silent films, Buck was a good actor. He was just as popular in talkies as he had been in silent movies. When the first list of Top Ten Western Stars came out in 1936, Buck Jones was Number One.

During the 1930s, Buck and his horse, Silver, starred in serials as well as series movies. One of his favorite leading ladies was Dorothy Fay, who later married singing cowboy Tex Ritter.

In 1941 Buck starred in *Arizona Bound*, the first of eight "Rough Riders" movies. The popular Rough Riders series co-starred Tim McCoy and Raymond Hatton.

In 1942 Buck attended a party given for him at the Coconut Grove nightclub in Boston. A fire broke out, and nearly 500 people were killed. As brave as any of his film heroes, Buck died trying to save his friends. A friend wrote to Buck's widow: "He was no less a hero to me—to all of us—than to the many, many children who worshipped him."

Buck Jones with leading lady Dorothy Fay.

Col. Tim McCoy

Col. Tim McCoy
He Wanted to be a Cowboy

Tim McCoy was born in Michigan in 1891. Like many boys he wanted to become a cowboy. When he was sixteen he saw the Miller Brothers 101 Ranch Wild West Show. Excited by the thrilling Wild West performers, Tim bought a train ticket to Wyoming.

In Wyoming Tim found work on cattle ranches. He learned to ride and rope. He saved his money and later bought his own ranch.

Tim met Arapahoe and Shoshone Native Americans in Wyoming. He became an expert on their history, and he learned their sign language.

During World War I, Tim joined the U.S. Army. He became a cavalry captain. He returned to his Wyoming ranch after the war and was appointed adjutant general of Wyoming troops.

In 1922 the first epic Western movie, *The Covered Wagon*, was filmed. Almost 1,000 extras were hired, including 750 Native Americans, and Tim McCoy was hired to help. Tim McCoy found work in other Westerns. Soon he was starring in his own movies.

As a Western star Tim already knew about cowboy work, Native Americans, and the U.S. Cavalry. He rode a white horse named Pal. He starred in a popular trio series, the Rough Riders, with Buck Jones and Raymond Hatton.

When the United States entered World War II, the Western star again served his country. He left Hollywood to become a colonel in the army.

The little boy who wanted to be a cowboy grew up to be a cowboy movie star. And in real life Col. Tim McCoy was a patriot who served his country in two world wars.

Bob Steele

Bob Steele
Fast and Furious

Bob Steele was an action star whose fast-paced and exciting films were filled with ferocious fight scenes.

His real name was Robert N. Bradbury, Jr. Bob had a twin brother named Bill. When Bob and Bill were boys, their father, a director, filmed them on hunting and fishing trips. Later their father released sixteen short films called *The Adventures of Bill and Bob*.

Bob's best friend was a tall youngster named Duke Morrison. Bob and his father helped Duke start in the film business. Duke later became John Wayne, the greatest of all Western stars.

In 1927, at the age of twenty, Bob changed his name to Bob Steele. For the next couple of years he starred in silent Westerns. Bob easily made the switch to sound films because he had a good speaking voice. Although he was short, he was strong and athletic.

There was little humor in Bob Steele movies. Bob developed a hero who was brave and fierce. He always faced larger villains who often knocked him down, but Bob always jumped up and whipped the bad guys.

Because he had a twin brother, Bob often played twins in his films. Or he played two characters who looked alike—a good guy and a bad guy.

During the 1930s, Bob's father directed several of his films. In 1940 Bob starred in six Westerns as Billy the Kid. Bob also played one of the "Three Mesquiteers" in thirteen films. Although his starring days ended in the 1940s, Bob continued to play smaller parts in the 1950s.

His friend John Wayne found parts for him in such 1960s movies as *The Comancheros* and *McClintock!* In 1968 a new star, Clint Eastwood, hired him for *Hang 'Em High*. When his old fans saw Bob Steele in these movies, they remembered a tough hero who was a whirlwind of action.

The Durango Kid

Charles Starrett
The Durango Kid

Charles Starrett was a big, handsome football star who easily became a cowboy movie hero. Charles was an outstanding fullback for Dartmouth during the 1920s. In 1924 a movie titled *The Quarterback* was filmed on the Dartmouth campus. Charles and some of his teammates were given small parts.

After that, Charles was bitten by the acting bug. He graduated from Dartmouth and headed for New York to act on Broadway. In 1930 Charles signed a movie contract. He appeared in non-Western films for five years.

In 1935 Charles was hired by Columbia Studios to film Westerns. During the next seventeen years Charles made 132 movies for Columbia. In 1937 he was voted one of the Top Ten Western Stars. Charles Starrett made the Top Ten list for fifteen years.

The Sons of the Pioneers provided music for many Charles Starrett films. Roy Rogers, an original member of the Sons of the Pioneers, had small parts in several Charles Starrett movies. From 1945 to 1952, the hilarious Smiley Burnette was Charles' sidekick.

In 1940 Charles filmed *The Durango Kid*. Charles played a cowboy named Steve. When villains caused trouble, Steve would disappear. He would reappear as the Durango Kid, dressed in black and wearing a black mask. The Durango Kid rode a white Arabian horse called Raider.

The Durango Kid was a mysterious, Zorro-like hero.The furious action in those movies mixed with comedy from Smiley Burnette. Charles Starrett made fifty-nine exciting Durango Kid movies before retiring in 1952.

The Three Mesquiteers. Left to right: Max Terhune (as Lullaby Joslin), Robert Livingston (Stony Brooke), and Ray "Crash" Corrigan (Tucson Smith).

The Three Mesquiteers

The Three Musketeers, a novel written by Alexandre Dumas in 1844, introduced the French musketeers as classic adventure heroes. A Western version of *The Three Musketeers* was created by American novelist William Colt MacDonald. In 1933 MacDonald began writing a series of Western novels about the "Three Mesquiteers."

In 1935 the first of many Mesquiteers movies was filmed, entitled *The Three Mesquiteers*. The Three Mesquiteers were named Stony Brooke, Tucson Smith, and Lullaby Joslin. Stony and Tucson were cowboy heroes, and Lullaby was their sidekick. All of the Mesquiteers could ride and fight. Stony and Tucson were strong and handsome, and often competed for the same girl.

Through the years the Three Mesquiteers were played by ten combinations of actors. The most familiar combination was Bob Livingston as Stony, Ray "Crash" Corrigan as Tucson, and Max Terhune as Lullaby.

Bob Livingston was a handsome actor. He later played the Lone Ranger in films.

The muscular, smiling Ray Corrigan began as a stuntman. Ray's falls from horseback earned him the nickname "Crash." He built Corriganville, a large movie set near Hollywood where countless Westerns were filmed.

Max Terhune was a ventriloquist. He had a dummy named Elmer. Max dressed Elmer in Western clothes. Max and Elmer added a lot of humor to Three Mesquiteers movies.

Other famous Western actors who played Mesquiteers included Bob Steele and John Wayne. John Wayne played Stony in a series of

Another trio of Mesquiteers. Left to right: Raymond Hatton (as Lullaby), John Wayne (Stony), and Ray Corrigan (Tucson).

eight Mesquiteers films. Ray "Crash" Corrigan continued to play Tucson. Lullaby was later played by a grizzled character actor, Raymond Hatton. The John Wayne films were among the best in the Three Mesquiteers series. Republic Studios produced these exciting movies.

Other studios copied the Three Mesquiteers. The Trail Blazers, the Rough Riders, and the Range Busters were trios like the Three Mesquiteers. Ray Corrigan and Max Terhune were hired to play two of the three Range Busters. But none of the other trios were as popular as the Three Mesquiteers.

Filmed through the 1940s, the Three Mesquiteers was one of the most popular series ever enjoyed by young Western fans.

Bad guy Roy Barcroft

The Bad Guys

Where would Western films be without the dangerous villains who threatened opposition to the heroes? The villains, also called "bad guys" and "heavies," were usually big and strong. They often wore black hats and mustaches. They were bullies who tried to pick fights with the hero. The hero often had to fight three or four bad guys at once.

Movie audiences knew the names of Western stars and their sidekicks. Young fans did not know the names of the villains. But the same actors played bad guys in hundreds of Western films. These tough-looking heavies were bad guys in one movie after another, week after week.

Young fans might not know their names, but they did recognize the bad guys as soon as they appeared onscreen. During silent movies some fans would boo when they recognized a bad guy. When two, three, or four recognizable villains appeared in a single movie, young fans knew that their hero was in for a tough time.

Roy Barcroft was called "King of the Heavies." He played the villain in more than 200 Westerns. Charles King and Warner Richmond were rugged bad guys in hundreds of silent films and talkies. Glenn Strange played the Frankenstein monster as well as hundreds of Western villains. Bud Osborne, George Chesebro, Edmund Cobb, and Earl Dwire also played hundreds of bad guys.

They may have been nameless, but everybody knew that they were mean and tough and needed to be whipped by the hero.

Wild Bill Elliott

Wild Bill Elliott
A Peaceable Man

"I'm a peaceable man."

This line was spoken again and again by Wild Bill Elliott. In one movie after another Wild Bill would try to avoid trouble. Then this "peaceable man" would be forced to fight.

Gordon Elliott was born on a Missouri farm in 1904. He learned to ride as a boy. He tamed horses while working at his father's stockyards. For a time he participated in rodeos.

But Gordon was interested in acting. He studied at the Pasadena Playhouse in California. By the mid-1920s Gordon was acting in silent movies. For years only a few of his films were Westerns.

In 1938 Gordon starred in a serial, *The Great Adventures of Wild Bill Hickok*. Gordon was tall and lean and looked good in Western clothes. Like Hickok, he wore his six-guns with the handles pointing forward. These reversed six-guns became a trademark of Elliott's costume.

Elliott was a hit as Wild Bill Hickok. He changed his name to Wild Bill Elliott, and soon played Hickok in a series of Westerns.

By 1940 Wild Bill was one of the Top Ten Western Stars. He was in the Top Ten for the next fifteen years, until the list was discontinued.

Wild Bill modeled his character on William S. Hart and Buck Jones. He was like his screen character—quiet but tough.

Elliott filmed another series about Wild Bill Hickok, and his co-star was Tex Ritter. Wild Bill also starred in a series about the popular comic strip cowboy, Red Ryder. The companion of Red Ryder was Little Beaver, a Native American boy. Wild Bill tried to include children in all of his films.

Wild Bill Elliott may not have really been "a peaceable man," but he was a very popular Western star.

More Stars of the 1940s

Western actor Ronald Reagan later was elected president of the United States.

Six-foot-six Sunset Carson was a rodeo performer who became a Western star during the 1940s.

Allan "Rocky" Lane played Red Ryder and other cowboy heroes during the 1940s.

Don "Red" Barry was another Western star of the 1940s.

Gene Autry's Ten Commandments of the Cowboy

1. A cowboy never takes unfair advantage—even of an enemy.

2. A cowboy never betrays a trust.

3. A cowboy always tells the truth.

4. A cowboy is kind to small children, to old folks, and to animals.

5. A cowboy is free from racial and religious prejudices.

6. A cowboy is helpful, and when anyone is in trouble he lends a hand.

7. A cowboy is a good worker.

8. A cowboy is clean about his person and in thought, word, and deed.

9. A cowboy respects womanhood, his parents, and the laws of his country.

10. A cowboy is a patriot.

The Singing Cowboys

The Old West left strong music traditions. The pioneers sang and danced to folk music for entertainment. Cowboys sang ballads to keep their cattle relaxed at night. When sound was added to Western films, the music came naturally.

Ken Maynard and John Wayne were among the first Western stars to use cowboy music in their movies. But Gene Autry was the first Singing Cowboy star.

The next Singing Cowboy star was Tex Ritter. Then the talented Roy Rogers became the King of the Cowboys. During the 1940s there were many other Singing Cowboys.

Republic Studios made the best Western films. Republic helped make a star of Gene Autry and Roy Rogers, and developed the last Singing Cowboy, Rex Allen.

During the 1950s, studios stopped making B Westerns and Singing Cowboy movies. But the Singing Cowboys had added color and fine music to many Western films.

Gene Autry

Gene Autry
The First Singing Cowboy

Gene Autry introduced a new type of cowboy hero to the movies. He made the Singing Cowboy popular and took Western films in a fresh direction. His musical Westerns were huge hits.

Gene was born in Texas in 1907. His father was a farmer. Gene's grandfather was a Baptist preacher who needed choir members. His grandfather taught little Gene to sing in the church choir. Gene later learned to play the guitar.

The Autry family moved to Oklahoma. Gene got a job on radio station KVOO in Tulsa. He became known as "Oklahoma's Singing Cowboy."

Soon he moved to a larger radio audience in Chicago. He was a singer on the "National Barn Dance" on station WLS. Gene started working with a talented musician named Smiley Burnette, who later would be Gene's movie sidekick. Gene began to record hit songs, such as "The Yellow Rose of Texas."

Next Gene decided to try the movies. Ken Maynard was adding cowboy music to his films, but he was not a very good singer. In 1934 Gene and Smiley sang in two Ken Maynard films, *In Old Santa Fe* and *Mystery Mountain.*

Then Gene starred in a serial, *The Phantom Empire*. This film mixed music and science fiction with Western adventure. Gene played a radio singer named Gene Autry. *The Phantom Empire* was a sensation.

Republic Studios began making musical Westerns starring Gene. His character was always named Gene Autry, and he often played a radio singer. Gene rode Champion, "The World's Wonder Horse." His movies usually were set in the modern West. Gene and Champion would sometimes gallop after gangsters who were driving a car.

Young villains wanted to believe that adventure was still possible in the West. Since there really was a radio singer named Gene Autry, his stories seemed believable. Gene was pleasant and friendly. To young fans he seemed like an older brother.

Gene's popularity soared. The Oklahoma town where he had lived even changed its name to Gene Autry. He received 80,000 fan letters each month, more than any other Hollywood star. In 1937 he became Number One among the Top Ten Western Stars. Gene was Number One for six straight years, until he volunteered for military duty in World War II.

In between movies, Gene toured across America. His fans came to see him at rodeos and fairs. Gene brought Champion and Smiley Burnette on tour with him. There were Gene Autry comic books and *Gene Autry's Melody Ranch* radio shows. His theme song was "Back in the Saddle Again." Gene recorded many popular Western songs, but his most successful recording was "Rudolph the Red-Nosed Reindeer."

After the United States entered World War II, Gene left the movies to join the U.S. Air Force. He served for four years as a transport pilot.

While Gene was gone from Hollywood, Republic promoted Roy Rogers as "King of the Cowboys." Roy became Number One on the Top Ten Western Stars list. But fans remembered Gene. After he returned to Hollywood in 1946, his first movie was *Sioux City Sue*.

Gene starred in more than ninety movies. In 1953 he made his last film, *Last of the Pony Riders*. But Gene had become interested in television. From 1950 through 1956, he starred in *The Gene Autry Show*. Gene's production company, Flying A productions, filmed these TV shows. Gene was the first movie star to film a TV series. His sidekick on television was Pat Buttram.

Gene's Flying A Productions also filmed such Western TV series as *The Adventures of Champion*, *Annie Oakley*, *The Range Rider*, and *Buffalo Bill, Jr.*

Gene had become wealthy from movies, records, and television. He retired as a performer to manage his business interests. But fans never forgot the first Singing Cowboy.

Tex Ritter
America's Most Beloved Cowboy

After Gene Autry became a star, Hollywood wanted more Singing Cowboys. In New York City a talent scout found a tall Texan who would become "America's Most Beloved Cowboy."

Woodward Maurice Ritter was born in 1905 and raised on a Texas farm. He learned to sing in church, and when he attended the University of Texas he was president of the Glee Club. After five years of college, Woodward went to New York to seek a career in show business. Because of his Texas accent, New Yorkers called him "Tex."

Tex Ritter appeared on Broadway, acting and singing in Western musicals. Tex also acted and sang on radio shows. In 1936 the popular cowboy actor signed a movie contract and moved to Hollywood.

Hollywood stuntmen taught Tex the tricks of screen fighting. Tex was big and strong, and his exciting fights with villains became highlights of his films.

Tex also was a fine horseman. In his movies he rode a big, white stallion named White Flash. Tex often was filmed in closeup, so that his fans could see that their hero—not a stuntman—was galloping aboard White Flash.

During his college days in Texas, he had collected Western songs from old cowboys. In addition to singing these real cowboy ballads, Tex wrote many songs for his movies. He played the guitar and sang in a deep, rich voice. Tex Ritter offered more authentic Western music in his movies than any other Singing Cowboy.

As a boy, Tex had enjoyed the silent movies of Hoot Gibson. Hoot was his favorite cowboy star. Like Hoot, Tex used a lot of humor in his films.

Tex Ritter movies became very popular. Between films Tex and

Tex Ritter

White Flash traveled all over America, appearing before their fans. Year after year, Tex was voted one of the Top Ten Western Stars.

In his 1937 film *Tex Rides With the Boy Scouts*, Tex used a Boy Scout troop from Los Angeles to help him solve a mystery. Boy Scouts everywhere identified with this movie.

Tex liked to use Native Americans in his movies, instead of actors dressed as Indians. For his 1940 film *Arizona Frontier*, Tex hired Native American Jim Thorpe, the most famous athlete in the world.

In 1940 Tex married one of his leading ladies, the beautiful Dorothy Fay Southworth. Tex and Dorothy Fay later had two sons, Tom and John. Tom Ritter would become a lawyer. Like his parents, John Ritter became an actor, starring in the popular television series, *Three's Company*.

In ten years Tex made sixty films for five movie studios. In a series of movies for one studio, Tex co-starred with Wild Bill Elliott. In another series he co-starred with Johnny Mack Brown.

Tex Ritter signing autographs for young fans.

By the time Tex stopped making films in 1945, he was a recording star for Capitol Records. Tex recorded cowboy ballads, religious music, and children's songs. He recorded more than 440 songs.

One of his biggest hits was the ballad for the 1952 movie *High Noon.* This famous film starred Gary Cooper, and a major reason for the success of *High Noon* was Tex Ritter's music.

For most of the 1950s Tex hosted *Town Hall Party*, a television show from Los Angeles. In the 1960s he moved to Nashville, where he became a member of the Grand Ole Opry. He was voted into the Country Music Hall of Fame in 1964.

Tex continued to perform until he died of a heart attack in 1974. During a career of nearly fifty years, Tex Ritter had performed on Broadway, on radio, in the movies, on television, on records, and on personal appearance tours. He truly had become America's Most Beloved Cowboy.

Roy Rogers and Trigger

Roy Rogers
The King of the Cowboys

Roy Rogers was "The King of the Cowboys."

His wife, Dale Evans, was "The Queen of the West."

His golden palomino, Trigger, was "The Smartest Horse in the Movies."

His bewhiskered pal, Gabby Hayes, was the best comic sidekick in Hollywood.

His musical partners, the Sons of the Pioneers, were the finest group of Western singers in the movies.

Needless to say, with this combination, Roy Rogers' films attracted huge audiences. And even after Roy Rogers stopped making movies, to fans he always remained "The King of the Cowboys."

Born Leonard Slye in 1911, he was raised on an Ohio farm. Len hunted and fished to put food on his family's table. He became an excellent shot.

Len's family loved music. Len grew up singing, yodeling, and playing the guitar. With his family he performed at dances. Len began to dream of a career as a performer.

The Slye family moved to California in 1931, and Len began to work as a singer. With Bob Nolan and other friends, Len organized the Sons of the Pioneers. Len sang and yodeled and played the guitar. This talented singing group started recording Western songs.

The Sons of the Pioneers made film appearances with Gene Autry, Charles Starrett, and other stars. Len began to play small parts in the movies of Autry and Starrett. When Republic Studios decided to find a new singing cowboy, Len was selected.

The name of the new star was changed to Roy Rogers. Roy found a

Roy Rogers with Dale Evans and Gabby Hayes.

movie horse named Golden Cloud and changed the palomino's name to Trigger. Trigger could perform dozens of tricks and could run very fast. Roy would ride Trigger in all of his movies and all of his TV shows. When he went on tour with Roy, Trigger loved to perform for fans.

Roy starred in his first movie, *Under Western Stars*, in 1938. In his early movies he played such historical Westerners as Billy the Kid, Jesse James, Buffalo Bill Cody, and Wild Bill Hickok. But soon Roy began to play himself in his films. Like Gene Autry, Roy's movies were set in the modern West.

Then the head of Republic Studios saw the musical *Oklahoma* on Broadway. He wanted to film Broadway musical scenes in Roy Rogers' movies. Roy began dressing in fancy costumes. His movies were filmed in color. There were wonderful songs and many dancers. The Sons of the Pioneers, now led by Bob Nolan, added their Western sounds to Roy's music. Audiences also loved the comedy of sidekick Gabby Hayes.

In 1942 Gene Autry joined the Air Force. Gene had been the Number One Western Star. By 1943, Roy was Number One. He remained Number One for twelve years, until the Top Ten Western Stars were no longer listed.

Beautiful Dale Evans first co-starred with Roy in 1944. She was the leading lady in twenty-eight of Roy Rogers' films. Roy's first wife, Arlene, had died following the birth of their third child in 1946. In 1947 Roy and Dale married.

Roy and Dale were strong Christians who raised a large family. Roy liked to end his radio shows or public appearances by saying, "May the good Lord take a likin' to you."

Roy starred in nearly ninety movies. From 1951 to 1957, *The Roy Rogers Show* was a popular TV series. The series was set on Roy's Double R Bar Ranch. Dale and Trigger co-starred, along with Roy's German Shepherd dog, Bullet. Comedy was provided by Pat Brady and his jeep, Nellybelle.

The theme song of Roy and Dale was "Happy Trails to You." Years after film and TV work, they continued to perform while stressing Christian values.

"The King of the Cowboys" set an example for his fans for sixty years. Roy Rogers and Gene Autry both died in 1998.

Dorothy Fay acted in Tex Ritter movies, then married Tex.

Leading Ladies

Cowboy heroes needed someone to rescue. Sometimes they rescued children or elderly people. But Western movies usually worked best when a pretty girl was threatened by villains. When a leading lady was rescued by a handsome cowboy, romance would certainly follow.

Western leading ladies were not helpless. They were brave and could shoot. Sometimes they helped the hero battle the villains. Actresses who specialized in Westerns had to be good riders.

Jennifer Holt was the leading lady in thirty-eight Westerns of the 1940s, more than any other actress. Her father, Jack Holt, had starred in silent Westerns. Her brother, Tim Holt, was a Western star during the 1940s.

Peggy Stewart was a beautiful brunette who played the heroine in many Republic Westerns. During the 1940s, she was the leading lady for Sunset Carson, Wild Bill Elliott, Rocky Lane, Charles Starrett, Roy Rogers, Gene Autry, and other cowboy heroes.

Marie Windsor was an award-winning horsewoman. She began appearing in Westerns during the 1940s. Marie had many other Western roles during the 1950s, 1960s, and 1970s. Instead of a heroine, she often played a villainess.

Peggie Castle was a beautiful blonde who played in Westerns during the 1950s. Peggie was the star of *Two Gun Lady* and *The Oklahoma Woman*. Later she co-starred in the television series *Lawman*.

Barbara Stanwyck was one of Hollywood's greatest actresses. She starred as *Annie Oakley* in 1935, *The Maverick Queen* in 1956, and in many other fine Westerns. On television she starred for four years in the popular series *The Big Valley*.

Dorothy Fay Southworth learned to ride on her father's Arizona ranch. She became interested in Westerns when a Tom Mix movie was filmed on the ranch. She studied acting in college. As Dorothy Fay she was the leading lady for Buck Jones, Wild Bill Elliott, and Tex Ritter. She and Tex fell in love and married in 1941. Dorothy Fay then left films to be a wife and mother.

Dale Evans also married her co-star, Roy Rogers. Dale was a lovely blonde with a beautiful singing voice. She was the leading lady in twenty-eight of Roy Rogers' movies. Dale's horse was named Buttermilk. The only leading lady with a famous horse, Dale was called "The Queen of the West."

Peggy Stewart

The Sidekicks

Comedy makes a story more entertaining. In the Western movies of the 1930s and 1940s, comedy was provided by the heroes' sidekicks.

The most famous Western sidekick was Gabby Hayes. Born in 1885, George Hayes spent twenty-five years as a stage actor. He moved to Hollywood and began to act in Westerns in the 1930s. During the next twenty years, George appeared in more than 130 Western movies. He was the bad guy in early John Wayne Westerns.

When he grew older, he lost his teeth and sported a white beard. As Gabby Hayes he was a whiskered, toothless old-timer. He became a sidekick for Hopalong Cassidy, Wild Bill Elliott, and Roy Rogers. Gabby appeared in forty movies with Roy Rogers. Young fans looked forward to Gabby's calling the bad guys "gol durn polecats." In 1945 Gabby was Number Two among the Top Ten Western Stars (Roy was Number One). He remained one of the Top Ten Western Stars for ten years.

Another sidekick who regularly made the Top Ten list was Smiley Burnette. Smiley went to Hollywood as Gene Autry's sidekick, and played that part in eighty-one movies. He also was the sidekick in sixty-four Charles Starrett films and in seven Roy Rogers movies. Smiley played fifty musical instruments and composed 300 songs.

As a character named "Frog," Smiley dressed in a floppy black hat and a checkered shirt. In a few films Frog had his own sidekick, a boy named "Tadpole." Tadpole also wore a floppy black hat and a checkered shirt.

There were other talented sidekicks. Raymond Hatton started in silent films. During his long career he was a sidekick in forty-five Johnny Mack Brown movies. Fuzzy Knight also was Johnny Mack

Gabby Hayes

Gene Autry with sidekick Smiley Burnette, and Smiley's sidekick, Tadpole. Smiley's horse was Ring-Eyed Nellie, and Tadpole also had a ring-eyed horse.

Brown's sidekick. Fuzzy was the sidekick for Tex Ritter and other cowboy stars.

Al St. John played a sidekick named "Fuzzy Q. Jones" in many Westerns. Max Terhune and his dummy, Elmer, were sidekicks for the Three Mesquiteers, the Range Busters, and Johnny Mack Brown.

Other sidekicks brought laughter to Western movies. Young fans loved the funny appearance and crazy behavior of Gabby, Smiley, and the rest of the Western sidekicks.

Rex Allen and Koko

Rex Allen
The Arizona Cowboy

The last Singing Cowboy was tall, handsome Rex Allen. Rex was from Arizona. As a boy he learned to play the guitar and to sing in church choirs. When Rex left high school, he sang on radio programs and performed at rodeos.

Republic Studios had brought Gene Autry, Roy Rogers, and many other cowboy heroes to the movies. The studio was impressed by the good looks and deep voice of Rex Allen. Rex signed a contract to star in musical Westerns for Republic.

His first movie, *The Arizona Cowboy*, was filmed in 1950. Roy Rogers, Republic's "King of the Cowboys," filmed an introduction to the first Rex Allen movie.

Rex bought a beautiful stallion named Koko. Koko was dark colored with a white mane and tail. He was trained by the same person who had taught Trigger, Roy Rogers' horse. Koko was called the "Wonder Horse of the Movies."

But by 1954 the studios stopped making musical Westerns. Rex and Koko traveled half a million miles across America to perform at rodeos and fairs. In 1958 Rex starred on television in *Frontier Doctor*. He narrated more than 150 nature films for Walt Disney Studios.

Rex Allen's fine entertainment career started because he was the last—and one of the best—of the Singing Cowboys.

Movies To See

Western heroes need to be seen in action to be appreciated. Old Western movies often appear on TV. A great many Western films are available on video.

I have listed two dozen fine Westerns that young viewers should enjoy. These are exciting movies with rousing action and magnificent Western scenery. Often a boy or girl is featured in the movie.

The Big Country (1958)	Gregory Peck*
The Cowboys (1972)	John Wayne
Dodge City (1939)	Errol Flynn
The Far Country (1955)	James Stewart
High Noon (1952)	Gary Cooper
Hondo (1953)	John Wayne
The Magnificent Seven (1960)	Yul Brynner
Man Without a Star (1955)	Kirk Douglas
My Darling Clementine (1946)	Henry Fonda
Night Passage (1957)	James Stewart
North to Alaska (1960)	John Wayne
Old Yeller (1957)	Fess Parker
Red River (1948)	John Wayne
Rio Bravo (1959)	John Wayne
Rio Grande (1950)	John Wayne
The Searchers (1952)	John Wayne
Shane (1953)	Alan Ladd
She Wore a Yellow Ribbon (1949)	John Wayne
The Sheepman (1958)	Glenn Ford
Silverado (1985)	Kevin Costner
Stagecoach (1939)	John Wayne
Three Godfathers (1948)	John Wayne
True Grit (1969)	John Wayne
Western Union (1941)	Randolph Scott

*movie (year released to theaters) star

Later Western Stars

Because Western movies were so popular, most of the important Hollywood actors made at least one or two Westerns. Some of the greatest Hollywood stars made many Westerns. These big-budget Westerns were greatly enjoyed by fans who had grown up watching B Westerns.

Gary Cooper was one of the greatest stars in Hollywood history. He was a superb rider and made many fine Westerns. James Stewart was another major film actor who starred in Westerns through the years. Ronald Reagan, future president of the United States, and Randolph Scott also starred in Westerns.

One of America's greatest war heroes, Audie Murphy, was a natural hero in Western movies. A more recent star to make Westerns is Clint Eastwood.

The greatest of all Western stars was John Wayne. One of Hollywood's most important actors, he starred in Westerns for more than forty years. John Wayne began in B Westerns, then made many of the best Westerns ever filmed.

Gary Cooper, here with Grace Kelly, won an Oscar for playing Marshal Will Kane in High Noon.

Gary Cooper
Marshal Will Kane

"When you call me that, smile!"

The most famous line in Western fiction was written by Owen Wister in his 1902 novel, *The Virginian*. The villain, Trampas, calls the Virginian a dirty name. The Virginian pulls a gun and tells Trampas, "When you call me that, smile!"

This line was first delivered on movie screens by Gary Cooper. Coop was raised on a Montana ranch. After breaking his hip, he rode horses very carefully because of the pain. He learned to anticipate every move his horse would make. Gary Cooper would be one of the finest horsemen in Western movies.

He arrived at Hollywood in the 1920s. Tall, lean, and handsome, Coop easily found work as a rider in silent Westerns. He rode as an outlaw or a Native American in several Tom Mix movies. Coop looked so good on-screen that he soon was given larger parts. He had important roles in several silent Westerns.

His first talkie was *The Virginian* in 1929. Male fans were impressed by Coop's strong, courageous image. Females loved his good looks and shy smile.

Gary Cooper became a movie superstar. He remained one of Hollywood's most important actors until he died in 1961. He won a Best Actor Oscar in 1941 for the title role in the war movie *Sergeant York*. There were many other outstanding performances in his non-Western films.

During his long career, Gary Cooper starred in about twenty Westerns. In 1936 he was a memorable Wild Bill Hickok in *The Plainsman*. Coop played other quiet, deadly Westerners in such fine films as *The Westerner* (1940), *Northwest Mounted Police* (1940), *Garden of Evil* (1954), *Vera Cruz* (1954), and *The Hanging Tree* (1959).

Coop's best Western performance was in *High Noon* (1952). He played Marshal Will Kane. Marshal Kane intended to turn in his badge on his wedding day. Just after his wedding, though, Kane learned that an outlaw gang was coming to town. The outlaw leader was a killer who had once been sent to prison by Kane.

No one in town was willing to help fight the four outlaws. Marshal Kane bravely stayed in town to meet the bad guys. The suspenseful movie ended with an exciting shootout between the marshal and the outlaws. Singing cowboy Tex Ritter sang the music for *High Noon*.

Gary Cooper won his second Best Actor Oscar for his portrayal of courageous Marshal Will Kane.

Randolph Scott
The Gentleman Hero

Randolph Scott was from Virginia. He was a true Southern gentleman. As a movie star Randy combined his courtly manners with heroic strength. A majority of Randy's 100 movies were Westerns. In his Westerns, Randolph Scott presented a polite but tough hero of the frontier.

When he was a young man, Randy left Virginia to study acting in Hollywood. Randy was tall and strong and looked good on a horse. He was given small parts in a few silent Westerns.

In 1929 he appeared in *The Virginian*, starring Gary Cooper. Since Randy was from Virginia, he gave Coop lessons on a Virginia accent.

Within a couple of years, Randy was starring in his own Westerns. In 1932 and 1933 he starred in nine films based on the Western novels of Zane Grey. The author was so popular that more than 100 movies were made from his novels. Randolph Scott's Zane Grey films made him a star.

Randy was a good actor who also starred in romantic movies and even musicals. But fans always enjoyed his Westerns.

In 1939 he played Wyatt Earp in *Frontier Marshal*. In many future films he would play heroic Western lawmen.

In 1941 Randy played a doomed outlaw in *Western Union*. The movie told the story of the first telegraph line built across the West. The character Randy played was on the wrong side of the law, but he was good at heart. Even when he played a bad guy, Randolph Scott turned out to be a hero.

A fine family man, Randy spent much time with his wife and two children. He loved to play golf, and exercised every morning to stay in

Randolph Scott

shape for his movies. His friends found him to be just as gentlemanly as his movie characters.

In 1942 he and John Wayne co-starred in *The Spoilers*. The story took place during the gold rush to Alaska. *The Spoilers* ended with a fist-fight between Randy and John Wayne. They put on one of the best fights ever seen in a Western movie.

By the 1950s Randolph Scott was making only Westerns, starring in three or four a year. Audiences looked forward to seeing his weather-beaten face with his quiet smile.

Randy retired after making *Ride the High Country* in 1962. It was one of the best Westerns ever filmed. Another fine Western actor, Joel McCrea, co-starred with Randy. In the end Joel and Randy shot it out with four outlaw brothers. One last time, Randolph Scott was a hero.

James Stewart in Winchester '73.

James Stewart
The Quiet Hero

James Stewart was a major star before he ever made a Western. In 1939 he played a lawman in his first Western, *Destry Rides Again*. The tall actor had a lanky build and an honest face. He spoke with a slow drawl. He seemed quiet and shy. People liked him and called him "Jimmy."

In 1940 he won an Oscar for Best Actor in *The Philadelphia Story*. He was one of Hollywood's most popular actors. During World War II, he joined the Air Force and became a bomber pilot. He won many medals for his courage in combat.

Jimmy was a hero in real life. Then he returned to playing Western heroes in 1950. His 1950 Westerns were *Winchester '73* and *Broken Arrow*. These fine films established the famous actor as a tough, stubborn Western hero.

During the 1950s and 1960s, Jimmy made Westerns with strong stories and beautiful scenery. In *Night Passage* another war hero, Audie Murphy, played his younger brother. Jimmy co-starred with John Wayne in *The Man Who Shot Liberty Valance*. Jimmy played Wyatt Earp in *Cheyenne Autumn*. He played a doctor in John Wayne's last film, *The Shootist*.

Jimmy Stewart was modest, likeable, and brave. Movie fans wanted to believe that they were like Jimmy. And in twenty Westerns he created believable frontier heroes.

Audie Murphy

Audie Murphy
Bravest of the Brave

Audie Murphy was a Texas farm boy. His father left the family when Audie was young, so Audie helped to feed his mother and his brothers and sisters by hunting. Audie shot rabbits and squirrels with a .22 rifle. His hunting skills would help him as a soldier.

Audie joined the U.S. Army when the United States entered World War II. He was still a teenager, and he was small. But he was an expert shot and had a hunter's instincts. For two years Audie battled Nazis in Europe.

Although Audie joined the army as a private, he was promoted to lieutenant. He was wounded three times. For his heroism, Audie was awarded the Congressional Medal of Honor. He was awarded many other medals and decorations for bravery. In fact, Audie was the most decorated soldier in the U.S. Army.

He wanted to stay in the army after the war, but his wounds made it impossible for him to pass the army's physical exam.

Audie was a natural for the movies. He had boyish good looks, and he was a popular hero. He soon became a star of action movies. Most action stars were much taller and larger than Audie. But audiences believed Audie in action movies because he was such a brave hero in real life.

In his first Western, Audie played Billy the Kid in *The Kid From Texas*. He played Jesse James in *Kansas Raiders*. *The Wild and the Innocent* was a comedy Western. Audie played a young pioneer whose sweetheart was a beautiful blonde actress, Sandra Dee.

Destry was an Audie Murphy remake of a 1939 Western that had starred James Stewart and, before that, Tom Mix. In one of his best roles Audie co-starred with Burt Lancaster in *The Unforgiven*. Audie and Burt were Texas ranchers who had to fight Kiowa warriors.

In addition to Westerns, Audie sometimes starred in war movies. His favorite role was as a young Civil War soldier in *The Red Badge of Courage*. In his most famous role Audie played himself in the World War II hit, *To Hell and Back*.

In his last film, *A Time for Dying*, Audie again played Jesse James. Most of Audie's forty-four movies had been Westerns.

In 1971, when he was forty-six, Audie was killed in an airplane crash. He was given a hero's burial at Arlington National Cemetery.

TV Stars
From the Big Screen To the Small Screen

Television sets began to appear in American homes during the late 1940s. Americans were used to seeing Westerns in movie theaters. It was natural for people to want to watch Westerns at home.

Because people stayed at home to watch television, movie audiences for B Westerns declined. By 1954 studios stopped making B Westerns. But old B Westerns were being shown on TV.

In the early 1950s *The Gene Autry Show* and *The Roy Rogers Show* brought the greatest Singing Cowboys to television every week. *The Lone Ranger* was another popular series. Then other Western series began to be filmed for television.

Adults as well as children enjoyed TV Westerns. Adults of the 1950s had grown up watching B Westerns when they were children. They were a ready-made audience for TV Westerns.

By the late 1950s more than half of the evening TV series were Westerns. A number of Western series were about the adventures of real Westerners, such as *Wild Bill Hickok*, *Bat Masterson*, and *Wyatt Earp*. When Walt Disney presented a series about Davy Crockett, boys all over America bought coonskin caps like Davy's.

Gunsmoke began in 1955. The star was a towering (six-foot-seven-inch) World War II hero, James Arness. Arness played Matt Dillon, a U.S. marshal in Dodge City. His best friend was Doc, and his sweetheart was Miss Kitty, who owned the Long Branch Saloon. *Gunsmoke* soon expanded from half an hour each week to an hour. The show was a fixture on television for twenty years. James Arness became one of America's greatest Western heroes.

Ward Bond was a familiar actor in many Western movies, especially

The Cartwright family of Bonanza. *Michael Landon (as Little Joe) is at top left, and Pernell Roberts (Adam) is beside him. Dan Blocker (Hoss) wears a ten-gallon hat at bottom, with Lorne Greene (Pa) beside him.*

The stars of Rawhide. *Left to right: Clint Eastwood (as Rowdy Yates), Paul Brinegar (Wishbone), and Eric Fleming (Gil Favor).*

The cast of Gunsmoke.
Top row, left to right:
Milburn Stone (as Doc Adams),
James Arness (Marshal Matt Dillon),
Amanda Blake (as Miss Kitty),
Ken Curtis (Festus).
Bottom row: Buck Taylor (Newly)
and Glenn Strange (Sam the bartender).

with his friend John Wayne. Big and loud, Ward starred every week on TV in *Wagon Train.* The old movie actor helped make *Wagon Train* one of the most popular shows on TV.

In 1959 *Bonanza* became the first Western series to be filmed in color. People were just starting to buy color TVs, and *Bonanza* was one of the few shows they could watch in color. *Bonanza* became one of the most popular shows on TV, running for fourteen years. The story was about the Ponderosa Ranch and its owners: Pa Cartwright and his sons, Adam, Hoss, and Little Joe. Little Joe was played by Michael Landon, who later starred in *Little House on the Prairie.*

The High Chaparral was another color series about a ranch run by a strong father figure. A similar series was *The Big Valley*, but the leader of this ranch family was the mother, played by Barbara Stanwyck. Earlier in her career she was the leading lady in many Western movies.

The popular novel and movie *The Virginian* also became the longest TV series. *The Virginian* ran for ninety minutes every week. James Drury played this classic Western hero.

James Garner starred as a Western gambler in *Maverick.* This series helped Garner become a major movie star. *Wanted: Dead or Alive* was about a bounty hunter in the Old West. Steve McQueen was the star, and he also became an important movie star. Another future movie star was Clint Eastwood, who played cowboy Rowdy Yates every week in *Rawhide.* Eastwood would go on to become the last great Western hero in the movies.

More than 150 Western series have been filmed for television. Many of the old TV Westerns, such as *Bonanza* or *Gunsmoke*, may be viewed on cable television. Television has carried on the tradition of the Western hero.

Clint Eastwood as The Outlaw Josey Wales.

Clint Eastwood
The Last Western Hero

Many old cowboy movie actors finished their careers by appearing in TV Westerns. But a few young actors began in TV Westerns and became Hollywood stars. Clint Eastwood would move from a TV Western to become a movie superstar.

When he was a young man, Clint served in the U.S. Army for two years during the Korean War. Clint was stationed in California. When he left the army, he studied acting in Hollywood.

Clint had small parts in a few Western movies. Then he was selected to co-star in a new TV Western, *Rawhide*. *Rawhide* told a new story each week about cowboys driving a cattle herd to the railroad. The trail boss was a character named Gil Favor. His "ramrod" (second-in-command) was Rowdy Yates.

Clint played Rowdy Yates for seven years, from 1959 through 1966. Clint was tall with rugged good looks. He spoke softly and played Rowdy as a friendly cowboy. Clint became very popular with TV audiences.

Then he went to Europe to star in a "Spaghetti Western," *A Fistful of Dollars*. This movie was a hit, so Clint filmed *For a Few Dollars More* and *The Good, the Bad, and the Ugly*. In these three movies Clint played "The Man With No Name," a gunfighter.

Clint had become a major movie star. He made detective films and other kinds of movies. But Clint returned to Westerns, which he usually directed. In *Coogan's Bluff* he starred as a lawman from the modern West who chases a criminal to New York City.

Hang 'Em High, *Joe Kidd*, *High Plains Drifter*, and *Outlaw Josey Wales* starred Clint Eastwood as a dangerous gunman. But he played a comical character in *Paint Your Wagon*, a musical Western about the California gold rush.

In 1992 Clint directed and starred in *Unforgiven*. He played a reformed killer who tried to support his family by farming. After his wife died, he had to hire out his guns to support his children.

Unforgiven won four Academy Awards. Clint won an Oscar for Best Director. *Unforgiven* received the Oscar for Best Picture. It had been more than sixty years since a Western won the Oscar for Best Picture. *Cimarron* in 1931 was the first Western selected as Best Picture. But Clint Eastwood finally made another Oscar-winning Western.

John Wayne
The Greatest Western Hero

"I don't act. I react."

This simple but effective acting technique was described by John Wayne. His response was convincing to other actors. And he worked to create a courageous, forceful heroic image.

John Wayne's career in films spanned nearly half a century. He made more than 150 movies. More than half of his films were Westerns. He starred in many of the best Westerns ever filmed. John Wayne became the greatest Western star in the history of film.

He was born in Iowa in 1907, but the family moved to California when he was a boy. His real name was Marion Michael Morrison. His dog was named Duke, and Marion was nicknamed "Duke." When he became a movie actor his name was changed to John Wayne, but his friends always called him Duke.

The big youngster grew to six feet, four inches and weighed more than 200 pounds. Duke was a football star at Glendale High School. Then he received a football scholarship to the University of Southern California in Los Angeles.

As a summer job Duke carried props for a movie studio. The tall prop man caught the eye of John Ford, one of the greatest directors in movie history. Ford tried Duke in a film, and found that he had a commanding screen presence. Another famous director, Howard Hawks, said that Duke "moved like a big cat."

After two years Duke dropped out of college and began work as an actor. He played several small parts. Then, in 1930, John Ford helped Duke get the starring role in *The Big Trail*, an expensive movie about a

John Wayne became a major star in Stagecoach.

wagon train. But John Wayne was too young and inexperienced to star in an important film. *The Big Trail* was a flop.

After the failure of *The Big Trail*, John Wayne could only find work in B movies. He starred in several Westerns directed by Bob Bradbury. Bradbury was the father of Duke's boyhood friend, a Western star named Bob Steele.

Duke played a cowboy named Singin' Sandy. But Duke could not sing, so Gene Autry would become the first singing cowboy. Duke also starred in a series of Three Mesquiteers movies.

During these years, Duke became a fine rider. The great stuntman Yakima Canutt taught Duke how to fight in a way that looked real onscreen. Duke learned to use his deep voice effectively. By the end of the 1930s, Duke was an experienced actor who had developed a heroic screen presence.

In 1939 John Ford filmed a thrilling Western, *Stagecoach*. Ford put his friend John Wayne in the role of the Ringo Kid. The film featured an exciting attack on the stagecoach by Apaches. The Ringo Kid helped fight off the Apaches, then shot it out with three outlaw brothers. *Stagecoach* was a hit, and John Wayne became a major star.

He was featured in adventure films as well as Westerns. During World War II, he played military heroes in war movies. The American people were looking for heroes during the war. Big John Wayne portrayed a hero that Americans wanted to believe in. He soon became America's top movie star.

John Wayne was the star of three superb Westerns about the U.S. Cavalry. These exciting cavalry movies were directed by John Ford: *Fort Apache*, *She Wore a Yellow Ribbon*, and *Rio Grande*.

Howard Hawks directed John Wayne in *Red River*. *Red River* was a magnificent movie about a cattle drive. In *Hondo*, John Wayne played Hondo Lane, a cavalry scout who had lived with Apaches. He starred in *The Searchers*, one of the finest Westerns of all time, directed by John Ford. John Wayne played a marshal fighting off outlaws in *Rio Bravo*.

John Wayne directed and starred as Davy Crockett in *The Alamo*. Then he starred in *North to Alaska*, one of the funniest Westerns ever filmed. He played a Texas Ranger in *The Comancheros*, and co-starred with James Stewart in *The Man Who Shot Liberty Valance*, directed by Ford.

During this period Duke discovered that he had cancer. A lung was

John Wayne starred as Hondo. *Co-starring were little Lee Aker, Geraldine Page, and Duke's close friend, Ward Bond.*

removed by surgery. John Wayne fans feared that their hero would die. But he recovered and soon began making films again. "I licked the Big C," said the Duke.

In 1969 he played Deputy U.S. Marshal Rooster Cogburn in *True Grit*. As Rooster he was tough and strong and funny. John Wayne was given the Best Actor Award for his memorable role as the old Western hero, Rooster Cogburn.

Another superb film was *The Cowboys*. John Wayne played a rancher who had to use schoolboys to drive his cattle herd. By this time John Wayne was the best-known movie actor in the world.

His last movie was *The Shootist*, filmed in 1976. John Wayne played an old gunfighter dying of cancer. At the start of *The Shootist*, gunfighting scenes from his earlier films were shown to portray him as a young man. Instead of dying in a sickbed, the shootist decided to die like a hero. He killed several bad guys before being killed himself.

Three years later, the Duke died of cancer. For decades he had played legendary Western heroes. John Wayne meant it when he said, "Nobody should come to the movies unless he believes in heroes."

Movie Words

B Western—a movie which ran about an hour. Because B Westerns were short, a theater usually ran two at a time in a **double feature** or **twin bill**. Many B Westerns were filmed in about a week on small budgets. Longer movies filmed on big budgets were **A Westerns**.

bad guys—also known as **villains**, or **heavies**. The bad guys caused a lot of trouble, but they were always stopped by the heroes.

closeup—a close view or camera shot of a movie character.

director—the person in charge of filming a movie. Western stars sometimes directed their own movies.

horse opera—a Western movie. Also called an **oater** or a **sage-brush saga**. A musical Western was called a **horse operetta**.

leading lady—a pretty actress who usually played the hero's sweetheart.

one-reeler—a reel of film takes about ten minutes to watch, and early movies were **one-reelers**, lasting only ten minutes. Then movies were expanded to **two-reelers**. Later movies were made up of several reels, lasting an hour or two.

Oscar—nickname for an Academy Award. Every year the Academy of Motion Picture Arts and Sciences awards Oscars for Best Picture, Best Actor, Best Actress, Best Director, and other achievements.

plot—the story told by the movie, written by a **screenwriter**.

Poverty Row—a neighborhood in Hollywood where small movie studios made cheap Westerns.

serial—a suspenseful movie directed into twelve to fifteen chapters. Each chapter was about ten minutes long. A new chapter was part of the movie program every week. At the end of each chapter the hero or leading lady faced fearful danger. Young fans could hardly wait until the next week's chapter to see what happened!

sidekick—the best friend of the hero. The sidekick usually was a comical character.

Singing Cowboy—hero of a musical Western. Also called a **tumbleweed troubadour** and a **saddlebag serenader**. A singing cowboy was as good with a guitar as a gun.

Spaghetti Western—a violent Western filmed in Italy or some other European country. The star was American, but the director and other actors were Italians.

stuntman—a fine horseman and athlete who performed riding tricks, falls from horses and buildings, and fight scenes.

talkie—a movie with sound.

ventriloquist—an entertainer with a dummy. The entertainer "throws" his voice so that the dummy seems to be talking. Ventriloquist Max Terhune and his cowboy dummy, Elmer, added comedy to many Western films.

Bibliography

Boswell, John, and Jay David. *Duke, The John Wayne Album.* New York: Ballantine Books, 1979.

Everson, William K. *A Pictorial History of the Western Film.* New York: The Citadel Press, 1969.

Garfield, Brian. *Western Films, A Complete Guide.* New York: Rawson Associates, 1982.

Hardy, Phil. *The Western.* New York: William Morrow and Company, Inc., 1983.

Hintz, H. F. *Horses in the Movies.* New York: A. S. Barnes and Co., Inc., 1979.

Holland, Ted. *B Western Actors Encyclopedia.* Jefferson, NC: McFarland Company, Inc., Publishers, 1989.

Hurst, Richard Maurice. *Republic Studios: Between Poverty Row and the Majors.* Metuchen, NJ: The Scarecrow Press, Inc., 1979.

Hyams, Jay. *The Life and Times of the Western Movie.* New York: Galbry Books, 1983.

Lyles, Allen. *The Western.* New York: A. S. Barnes and Company, Inc., 1975.

McClure, Arthur F., and Ken D. Jones. *Western Films, Heroes, Heavies and Sagebrush of the "B" Genre.* New York: A. S. Barnes & Company, 1972.

McDonald, Archie P., ed. *Shooting Stars, Heroes and Heroines of Western Film.* Bloomington: Indiana University Press, 1987.

Meyer, William R. *The Making of the Great Westerns.* New Rochelle, NY: Arlington House, Publishers, 1979.

Nicholas, John H. *Tom Mix, Riding up to Glory.* Kansas City, MO: The Lowell Press, Inc., 1980.

Place, J. A. *The Western Films of John Ford.* Secaucus, NJ: The Citadel Press, 1973.

Rainey, Buck. *Saddle Aces of the Cinema.* New York: A. S. Barnes & Company, Inc., 1978.

Ricci, Mark, and Boris and Steve Zmijewsky. *The Films of John Wayne.* New York: The Citadel Press, 1970.

Rogers, Roy, and Dale Evans. *Happy Trails, Our Life Story.* New York: Simon & Schuster, 1994.

Rothel, David. *The Singing Cowboys.* New York: A. S. Barnes & Company, Inc., 1978.

Scott, C. H. *Whatever Happened to Randolph Scott?* Madison, NC: Empire Publishing, Inc., 1994.

Tuska, Jon. *The Filming of the West.* Garden City, NY: Doubleday & Company, Inc., 1976.

———. *The Vanishing Legion: A History of Mascot Pictures, 1927–1935.* Jefferson, NC: McFarland & Co., Inc., 1982.

West, Richard. *Television Westerns.* Jefferson, NC: McFarland Company, Inc., 1987.

Witney, William. *Trigger Remembered.* Huntsville, AL: Golden Rule Printing, 1989.

Yoggy, Gary A., ed. *Back in the Saddle, Essays on Western Film and Television Actors.* Jefferson, NC: McFarland & Company, Inc., 1998.

Places To See

Tom Mix Museum
Dewey, Oklahoma

Gene Autry Museum of Western Heritage
Los Angeles, California

Roy Rogers–Dale Evans Museum
Victorville, California

Tex Ritter Museum
Carthage, Texas

Rex Allen Museum
Willcox, Arizona

National Cowboy Hall of Fame
Oklahoma City, Oklahoma

Old Tucson Movie Set
Tucson, Arizona

About the Author

Bill O'Neal's great-grandfather was a Texas cowboy, and his grandmother came to Texas in a covered wagon when she was a little girl in 1881. When Bill was a boy growing up in Texas, he learned to love the West by going to Western movies.

Bill now teaches Western history at Panola College in Carthage, Texas. He has written nearly twenty books about Western history and baseball. His books have covered ghost towns, gunfighters, and cattle ranches. One of his books is about Singing Cowboy movie star Tex Ritter. Bill's next book will be about the famous Western singing group, the Sons of the Pioneers.